Praise for *Phoenixbirds*

Delicately aware of the world seen and unseen, heard and unheard, the poems in Jane Dickerson's *Phoenixbirds* allow for simultaneous loss and transcendence. From the mechanics of an egret's flight to the image of the necks of long-necked swans, these poems, made of gorgeous sentences and well-cut lines, privy a world I want to inhabit. This is a book to experience again and again.

Sally Keith, author of *Two of Everything*

In this closely observed, thoughtfully orchestrated collection, Jane Dickerson explores the paradoxes of a life lived attentively: the steadying power of ephemeral nature, the sometimes baffling histories of families we love, the wound of raising a disabled child, and indeed, the woundedness of life itself. These are brave poems, shaped by the author's conviction that "It's a luxury to write/about a bird, any bird, when / the world is full of anguish."

James Silas Rogers, author of *The Collector of Shadows*

Simple truths told with a smart tongue. Be educated or bring your dictionary for you are about to learn english…a lovely and poignant english. And know your north American birds and flowers or learn them. animals and plants in this work are vital as the writer's ancestors, herself and her family…right up there with water and oxygen.

Even when sentimental, hard truths about our human race are exposed without scorn or judgment – the facts are allowed to speak for themselves, but precious are the birds and flowers that help carry or lift human indecencies.

Jane Dickerson's work pulls us underwater just long enough to sense how it must feel to drown in hearing loss, but also to live among brilliant living colors in every direction, even when a tree goes down "the space it had filled [was] filled with blue."

Don Farrell, author of *there are soft and beautiful things in this world – please find me*

These poems grapple with how to weather grief, grief over the loss of friends, family, species, habitat. A profusion of birds and flowers remind us of the necessity of joy. Jane Dickerson also reminds us to listen when we can't see and to see when we can't hear.

Athena Kildegaard, author of *Midden*

"It's a luxury to write/about a bird, any bird, when/the world is full of anguish." So writes Jane Dickerson in "Robin's Egg Blue." The homey robin parenting its nestlings in a sturdy, yet complex nest sits in stark contrast to the phoenix bird of the collection's title. After its long life, the phoenix goes out in a blaze of glory then rebirths itself from its own ashes. Yet both poems lead us to rebirth and a future. In poems, as well-crafted as the robin's nest, Dickerson takes on motherhood, adoption, language, deafness, and perception. Linger in them as you would in a sanctuary. Enjoy the profusion of species, color, and sound.

Morgan Grayce Willow, author of *Dodge & Scramble*

In these poems, Jane Dickerson "dips in & out" of "the plain, the odd-shaped, & lacquered jewels" of memories – of her parents & grandparents, her children, and her own agrarian childhood. She gives voice and insight into the world of the Deaf, and with a birder's sharp eye she enfolds us in nature, eliciting both a profound grief for earth's losses and an aching appreciation for the world as it is

Rita Moe, author of *Sins & Disciplines* and *Findley Place; a Street, a Ballpark, a Neighborhood*

Phoenixbirds

Minneapolis

First Edition July 2025
Phoenixbirds. Copyright © 2025 by Jane E. Dickerson
All rights reserved.

No parts of this book may be used or reproduced by any means, graphic, electronic, or mechanical, including photocopying, recording, taping or by any information storage retrieval system, without the written permission of the publisher except in the case of brief quotations embodied in critical articles and reviews.

10 9 8 7 6 5 4 3 2 1
ISBN: 978-1-962834-47-6

Cover and book design by Gary Lindberg

Phoenixbirds

Poems
Jane Dickerson

Minneapolis

Contents

I

Reverie at the Other Como 2
Home... 3
Handbook on Grief 4
The Widow's Mite 5
The Tree as It Died 6
In a Dream 7
Cloud 8
Climate Grief 9
Audiology 10
For Stan 12
Like Richly Colored Robes 13
Forfeiture 14
Teaching Religious Education at the Deaf School 15
The Poet Tells Her Adopted Children Stories 16
Dream of the Hard-of-Hearing Woman 18
A Mold of Lady's Paw 19
Paper-Whites 20
Waiting for Claire 21

II

How Still It Is Among the Trees 24
Drought 26
Inheritance 28
Urban Pond 29
Grief 30
Phoenixbirds 31
Some Move at Lower Elevations 32
The Phoebe 33
Another Drought 34
Meditation on Step Three 35
Thrift 36

The Pencil	37
Erasure	38
Late Snow & the Bird Feeder	39
Sketches	40
As the Crow Flies	43
Tankas & the Temperature	44
West Virginia: Pop Williams	46
Mirabile Dictu	47
Spring Song	48

III

Reservoir Woods in Low Light	50
Matrilineal	51
Rosemary	53
Moving on from the Graveyard	54
Legacy	55
Harry Runner & the Horse	56
West Virginia: Song	58
Claire: Mother's Day	59
My Mother's Hands	60
Man with a Hatchet	61
Counting Horses	62
The Opera Rocks	63
Robin's Egg Blue	64
In Holland	65
West Virginia: Landscape	66
On the Occasion of Your Birthday	67
Swans at Lake Johanna	68
Notes	69
Acknowledgements	70
About the Author	71

For My Father

"Plant a Garden in which strange plants grow
& mysteries bloom."
~Ken Kesey

Also by Jane Dickerson

The Orange Tree: Early Poems

1

Reverie at the Other Como

I'm glad to find my bench deserted,
the park, too, for that matter,
because it's a weekday & cloudy
& chill enough to stay the walkers,
though not the lovers who just strolled by.

The birds are scarce, not one wing
in the trees or on the lake,
in this city, where a century ago
someone thought to dig a lake & name
it for the one in Italy I doubt I'll see.

Here, under an awkwardly leaning pine,
my hope of finding any bird diminished,
equably decide it doesn't matter,
become philosophical, thankful,
for that which lies before, behind.

The other day an Easterner wrote
about a bird, to him mysterious,
finally deciding it was an Old World warbler.
Impossible. Did he see something wished for?
I've done that so many times.

Home...

is also the ruby-throat
       looking for sugar sap
in the fluted flower on the balcony,
       the black & orange oriole
that scoops the purple jelly & stabs
       the sliced fruit for sustenance,
& that slightly yellow bird beyond
       the green, hunting insects in the road,
the bird you recognize but cannot name
       or hear, but for the want of which
would be to know a diminution,
       another loss in your earthly home
because without them, you & the world
       are undone.

Handbook on Grief

I archived the link to the book.
I'll need it to tell me what to do
when I break down & how to recover.
I'm supposed to die before her,
my forty-year-old deaf daughter who
hopes to join the dogs & other pets in heaven,
the place she signs above her head
when she's able to raise her arms that high.
Her breasts were first to go & now her heart
is failing. She's taken the loss of male
attention like someone with her point of view:
after the double surgery, she smiled
for the camera in my phone, left hand
signing *I love you* for friends & family,
bald & proud in her blue pajamas.
She won't let me delete them.
I don't want to remember, but obey.

The Widow's Mite

Enchanted by a bird humming near,
speaking in a foreign tongue,
like an unrecoverable waking dream—
O, to understand its origin & end.

Among the flowers of attraction,
she stirs atoms of red & regency.
The clematis has unfurled itself,
jutting stamens from a yellow center.
I feel her tiny wings beat & buzz,

her little heart, wild & pulsing—
a lovely cipher, like the ancient
widow's mite, a gift beyond all
proportion, which confounds.

The Tree as It Died

That spring the tree put all its force in flowering,
as if by fecundity, the puny scalloped leaves,
the silver trunk & gray-green limbs,
could survive by dint of generosity.

The perfume of a thousand blooms filled the air,
& a throng of bees, bumping from bloom
to sticky bloom, all but drowned in it.
From the balcony I watched the dance—

first the intoxication of hope & then
the tired seeds: puny, round, & hard.
In autumn, a band of waxwings raided the tree,
their dipped-in-yellow tails flicking up & down,
& returned until it was reft of progeny.

The last, a storm that torqued the trunk
while in a darkened room we watched *Elektra*,
its lashing crescendos drowning both the storm
& the linden's crashing, till in morning we found
it felled, & the space it had filled filled with blue.

In a Dream

In a dream our daughter is gone—
an empty bed, pillows in the trunk.

Next, unsettled sleep, & in its place,
a fear of sleep, & finally no sleep at all.

She hasn't lived with us in twenty years.
When she visits, she chooses the narrow sofa.

What could it mean or have meant?

I see the comforter downturned,
the pillows in the trunk.

Has she made the break? Has she left us,
not we, her, at last?

Cloud

At the murky side pond of the lesser Langton Lake the day I looked for swallows—the dressy tree kind in their blue-black tux, the ochre-vested barn & the rough-winged—none skimmed the surface nor dove nor soared the way they do, aerialists on wing. But on the other shore, shadowed by prickly buckthorn, stood a bird as sublime as any summer cloud: A great white egret balanced on one black spindle leg, the three spidery toes of the other frozen mid-air, yellow disc eye gleaming. The crook'd neck sank an inch, then two, before the long beak darted & jerked back with a neon orange, eight-inch koi, flipped & caught midair. The feathered neck bulged with the koi's slow descent. In all, a ten-minute affair, & the white cloud drifted on.

Climate Grief

So that's what it's called, a catchall
for the sorrow I feel when I want
to take a walk, but it's too hot, too dry,
& the lake heading down to silt or
overtaken by lily pads so thick
the geese & ducks are stymied, but
sandpiper chicks can walk upon them,
easy prey for the red-tailed hawk.

Audiology

The young woman with the long brown hair
who checked my ears may have smiled
when I joked about my faded hearing,
my yearly dose of truth I'd said,
but who could tell the face she wore beneath
the blueish surgical mask tied behind her ears?
After an hour's worth of testing, it was clear
that even spondees like baseball, sidewalk, & salt lick
were lost on me, words ten years ago I could
have deciphered in the soundproof booth.

When Claire was that *infant in my arms*,
the graphed audiograms of what her nine-month
inner ears could sense were flat as pancakes—
that audiologist thought a locomotive might rouse her.
I was alone, lost for words as she slept.
Did this explain her restiveness & crying? We tried
not to compare her brother, adept & then some,
at everything for his age. The records I'd loved,
Woody's songs & the Italian concertos,
their faded yellow covers, became as nothing.

Before our isolation, the person who'd checked
my hearing, the one with the odd high-pitched bray,
said she'd never fit me in another set of aids,
pushed me to consider cochlear implants. I saw
a surgeon for information & then checked no
because deafness for the Deaf I know isn't
a basket of signs & meanings, but Life.
This day the woman with the blueish mask
said to wear my ten-year-old, behind-the-ears set
as long as they held up—praised their longevity.

For Stan
~1939-2019

Winter, an early jay arrives just out the window
& sets the hanging feeder swaying.
The bird steadies, beaks a seed, & teeters,
dumping the new snow in a flash of blue.
The jay you saw startled, delighted—

you hadn't seen or heard one in so long.
You'd become a city man,
had almost forgotten its sapphire hue,
its *queedle,* you wrote, its *complaint.*
I imagine your bird on a sunny day

the summer you saw it, in good light
that paints its feathers achingly.
Albeit air & sky are its elements,
if frightened one will take to the center
of any dense shrub or tree.

What took you, you believed, fell
like the dust of stars *into your mouth,*
airborne, aerial, floating, falling,
fell when you were born & waited
with considered patience

until you'd lived a long life
to show itself as the sidelong Crab,
also known as Cancer, dimmest
of the firmament's constellations,
most canny, most cunning.

Like Richly Colored Robes

~for Dick

Beautiful because unexpected,
catch-in-the-breath beauty,
like the long hedge of purple lilacs
you said last spring didn't know
the desolate part of town they grew in.
Like the weeds I carried home
from vacant lots when we were young—
the rank, the Queen Anne's lace,
that sky-blue chicory, the wild & branching
brown-eyed Susan I made a fist of.

Now, here, bordering a garden on this trafficked street,
half-a-dozen plants as big as shrubs weep
blood-red trains of ornamental amaranth
that drape themselves on magenta leaves
like the richly colored robes of new arrivals
in their otherworldly opulence—
startling in the urban catastrophe,
this orange & that gold, unforeseen
in what should be fall, a perfusion
of warmth, an ecstasy of color.

Forfeiture

Spring mornings, birders make their rounds, collecting
& documenting the palette-colored passerines,
warblers, & others of the perching family found
at the feet of the city's glassy, well-lit towers.
One day a dozen, the next fewer, or more, unless
an early scavenger—coyote, crow, or feral cat—finds
them first. The limp bodies, some not yet cool, with broken
necks & silent wings, are carried to the Bell Museum
of Natural History to be quietly stored in long, oaken
drawers with curved pulls on the second floor.
Migration is a noisy storm of warning chirps
& calls, & wings that pump for hours, sometimes
days on end, north from the Americas across the Gulf
on what's known as the Mississippi Flyway. A majesty
of flight that registers on radar & repeats for weeks.
From St. Paul many venture further north to arboreal
woods or the Arctic tundra where the horizon makes
an arc & insects swarm in multitudes, fare for the hatchlings,
until the call of change in late July sets waves of wings
clamoring south again toward urban towers where
the young are most apt to crash—the lights & glass
a novelty they can't discern along their pathway's corridor.

Teaching Religious Education at the Deaf School

Usually late for my classes, I drove over the limit,
afraid I wouldn't make it before the kids, alone & free,
trashed the classroom the school allotted me. This was
before I decided there wasn't much worth risking my life.

In winter, clutches of pines blocked some of the
snow that blew across the road & could slicken
to ice under the coldest sun. Over the years
the pines grew taller, thicker, & my students graduated,

a few pregnant, despite the lessons on sexuality
I held with the Lutherans, & another on the mechanics
led by a nurse who demonstrated the condom
& its use. Some left for Deaf colleges in DC or

upstate NY, others stayed in town & worked at the Deaf School.
One standout became a celebrated women's basketball player.
Some married, had children, & some, of course, divorced.
Some died, as well, like delicate Nicole who succumbed

to a congenital disease, & the kind & lovely Joan, whose
body was smashed by a hit-and-run driver on a bad
weather night in Apple Valley when she ventured out
to buy cat food. A dozen of my old students showed up

for the funeral in the small-town church further north,
the service in ASL for Joanie's friends & brother, wearing
their best pressed jeans & tees or party clothes, unfamiliar
with this ritual & the gasp of incense shaken over the coffin.

The Poet Tells Her
Adopted Children Stories...

The things your siblings laughed about—
the time the dog, not a rabbit, got caught
in the trap Joe, the boarder, fashioned with a box
& stick in your grandmother's garden between
the house & river, or your sister pulling the second-
story toilet chain & running just in time to
see where the pipe drained directly to the river
& watch what had been inside her fall into the current.

What you yourself remember about the mountains,
driving lost with your father for the fun of being lost.
Always, the ancient house you loved in Morgantown,
the pantry drawer full of pink candies & patterned feed-sacks,
now become a shopping mall at the end of town.
What your mother shared of her youth, graduating
young from high school, living with her parents
in the Depression, her younger brother, Harry Clyde Jr.,

dying from scarlet fever at twenty-three, then teaching
in a one-room country school till she married
& was forbidden by the rule of only one earner
in a family, the male, & the secrets she said she'd carry
to her grave & did, & you thinking, how terrible to
never tell a soul. What you knew of your father's past—
what he revealed to your mother about his childhood, or
how he called her "Darling" on a postcard sent from camp

in the second war, & once at the funeral, his youngest brother
saying how much your father loved to run the mountain trails,
lunch pail in hand, to work the mines before he left for college,
& then his running up another road, uncle Joe said,
your drunken grandfather, whom you never met, waving
a pistol not too far behind. You never thought they would die,
they lived so long. Some of it you told your children, culling
the stories you knew, or speculated, so they would know something
more about your own past's past, even if not entirely their own.

Dream of the Hard-of-Hearing Woman

Last night I dreamt the birds were singing,
copiously & loudly.

There was, of course, a porch & a swing.
The birds sounded

as I remembered them, sweet robin redbreasts
& cardinals in the trees,

which were dense & full-canopied.
Fantastically,

three big, orange-billed pelicans sat on the roof,
leisurely & kindly.

It was daytime. The air soft & damp,
without humidity.

When I woke, I thought about the pale green
swing, its faded pillow.

When I woke, it was a different world,
& I whistled

that song about heaven: *I'm in
Heaven.*

A Mold of Lady's Paw

The crude clay print of her forepaw,
too rough for paint or polish, was the vet's
idea of solace before they burned her.
We could have had her ashes, too,
for a price we couldn't conscion.
When, not if, Claire decided to dig them up,
could we have denied her? The coarse plaque
seemed disingenuous, unlike the handprints
made in grade school painted by children.
Claire carried the rough slab in her gym bag
for months till she stowed it a drawer—
a shrug when I wondered why.

Paper-Whites

~Narcissus papyraceus

Even the bulbs are papery, glossy brown &
onion-like, squeezing the sides of the creamer
& sugar bowl they're nested in.

My mother taught me how to force
them into bloom, a thing she learned
in her Southern garden club, where she was

doted on, I believe, because she was older,
& had a sharp shy wit that must have tickled them.
They called her Millie; old friends did not.

The Christmases I didn't make it home, she sent
me some to house in darkness till the roots took hold,
with instructions to move to sunlight once they did.

I find my own now, before the real dark sets in.
More than novelty in the lull of winter, the way
the bright crowns & faint yellow centers

tower on the windowsill, the way their white
breath drifts across the room, intoxicating, even
as they begin to desiccate, having no second life.

Waiting for Claire

What can I tell you about how much
I love my daughter? Where do I begin?
It's more than the width of my arms,
a thing she can understand.

Today she will be taken
from her home to the hospital,
where they think they can help her.
Her—more than a handful.

It's Ash Wednesday:
Forty days in a dry & arid land.
I have become so stupid.
I wash the floor before I go.

On my way across the city
to the countryside where she lives
the usual crow sits sentinel
topmost in a tree, & further on,

a red-tail rises from a limb.
Someone has planted pines
at intervals to thwart the snow,
its drift across the highway.

The road rends what's left
of *le bois grand*, the Big Woods,
once dense with oak & elm,
the fragrant linden & the giant maple.

Another day, she & I might walk
a larger remnant to the east,
leaves matted in the creek,
look for birds, & hold each other's

hand, hiking downhill to the falls
that trickle over the escarpment
where the stream begins. *Le bois grand*
ends in Nerstrand Woods south

of the Cities, where we see early drifts
of violets & the nodding anemone
that carpet the forest floor,
happy in our solitude.

II

How Still It Is Among the Trees

After my mother died, I walked the dog.
I walked a long distance, but not nearly
as far as the time she lived, nor the time
it took for her to die. I walked the dog
to the little grove of trees across the street
on the edge of the golf course, taking
the long way. I walked him down the road
early in the morning, just as it began
to lighten, before the stars went in.
I walked around the marsh pond
with its skin of ice, & the dog scared
the ducks, which rose as a raucous cloud
over the trees before veering toward town
& the river. We passed the new houses
by the pond, houses with unseeing eyes,
shiny in the new light. Then we crossed
another road & walked beyond the no trespassing
sign to the rustic little bridge & watched
the creek trickle to where we'd seen a rat plop in.
We walked on the snow's crust, unsolid frosting.
Among the pines, we stopped, & I listened
to familiar voices, the daily joggers on the road.
We stood among the trees until the sun
brightened, the dog pulling & sniffing
after scents. The boughs were coated with snow
& ice. It was quiet when the joggers
drifted off. I think I heard the birds begin.

Of course, I thought about her & how
little I could think or could remember,
except the way it was the last day I saw her,
a memory of the closed critical ward,
my mother, humbled, unmoving, only a tear
when I think she heard my voice beside her face,
& Mother, dear Mother, nearly gone, nearly ninety,
left to live another week, how still it is among the trees.

Drought

Next door the old man can't bend to pull the weeds,
& kills his dahlias with too much food.
His peas will not rise from the black dirt,
the chicken wire trellis standing free & bare.
But his lawn is green & thick,

watered daily in the drought,
& fine or no fine, no one turns him in—
the neighbor children run & wheel
through the artificial rain, the mist
evaporating cloudless in the heat.

And his roses flourish, tropically,
the thorns of the red climber catching
my arms & legs through the pickets,
& though I clip the runners, they grow back.
His wife doesn't remember she's shown me the house,

has told me before about his two heart-attacks,
that I've seen the vine tomato he grew from seed.
She tilts her head, shaking, watching him as she speaks.
In the fall I study the way he moves across the lawn,
his body cross-hatched by the leafless maple.

He neither shuffles nor trudges, but somewhere between,
not quite finished, but near, it looks to me.
Each day he goes more slowly,
though his voice is clear & strong when he tells me
how to dig a trench around my roses,

to cover the roots with leaves & straw for winter,
reminds me that before I lived here,
my lawn was blue with bugleweed,
the tiny flowers like a carpet,
advises bent grass like his grows fast & best.

Inheritance

Every woman had a box of buttons where
she stored the extras from the skirts, blouses, dresses,
& coats she sewed, saving them for years
until they were packed in bags for the Goodwill
when her house was cleared & emptied of her.
I know this is true because I handled more
than one woman's household laid out on the curb.
I don't know what happened to my mother's button box,
a rectangular affair that had held a crème-filled
chocolate egg & was decorated with small farm
animals in spring pastels. I played on the rug
by the sewing machine, dipping my hand
in & out, letting the plain, the odd-shaped,
& lacquered jewels slide through my fingers.
When I became an adult with children whose
clothes I sewed to kill the time while watching them,
I, too, kept buttons, dozens in a lidded basket, including
those I found among a woman's half-finished quilts.
One night at my parents' home my mother paid
me a compliment, then qualified the praise,
which piqued my father who'd snorted & said what
she'd done was like "taking the buttons off the coat."
She huffed a little, & I was filled with suspicion
when she said it meant to strip the buttons from
a garment before giving it away.

Urban Pond

~For Hayden Carruth

At Langton Lake it's a thrill
to see birds in spring—honking geese &
four white egrets distanced
each from the other within sight.
I can hope one will stay for summer.
But not one of the tall white birds stayed,
& none returned in fall to say good-bye
as far as I could see along the shore
of the twin lakes drying to a foot
below the cattails' water line,
red-eared turtles sunning
on a downed log in the shallows.

Grief

The museum pond is half-frozen   *(where a red-tailed hawk surveyed*
now, & across the road   *its demesne from the top of the*
the bur oaks,   *middle oak, its few dead limbs)*

the Norway maples further   *(the world's most gorgeous warbler*
south,   *once flitted there)*

the ginkgoes catacorner to   *(their leaves made a crisp sound*
Mim's Café,   *after a hard frost when, as one,*
   they fell)

& the sky-high cottonwoods on   *(one spring three brown creepers*
the old tram path have all   *picked their way around the trunks)*
been taken down.

Miles of rutted road from   *(Philando Castille was murdered*
Larpenteur to University are   *a mile east in his girlfriend's car,*
smoother, wider now.   *her daughter looking on)*

      Made-to-look-quaint streetlights
        punctuate the night, light
        the road, hide the stars.

Phoenixbirds

~For Ken Kesey on the death of his son, Jed, in 1984

The hardest part, he wrote the gang of friends
who couldn't make the funeral, was when
they'd had to sign the papers to let the doctor
harvest the boy's organs before his life had ended,
the boy whose brain had been dead for days
after the wrestling team bus floated off a cliff,
the boy whose skull his father had packed with fresh snow
in plastic bags in the hospital to slow the swelling,
the boy who seemed to show signs of life
just minutes before he flatlined, the boy whose box
they'd hand-built from pine with a lining the women stapled in—
a Tibetan brocade with gilded *phoenixbirds* —
& a satin pillow on which to rest his head made from the down
of a swan one of them had mistaken for a snow goose
& had buried quickly, but not before the plucking,
the boy whose kidneys the day he died saved *"two young somebodies,"*
in all, twelve parts of him passed on, including his perfect
corneas, a boy whose father wrote about the prayers they'd said,
the songs they'd sung & who ended the letter to his friends
and the red-winged blackbirds sing in the budding greengage plumtree
by way of showing how he was weathering his grief.

Some Move at Lower Elevations

The day I cleared the garden—the matted
frost-congealed vines tangled in the fence,
perfect-looking tomatoes gone soft at heart,
over-ripe beans beneath desiccated leaves—
a bird darted too fast to catch its color.

The Phoebe

I am burying the bird, grey as dawn,
in the upper bed along the drive.
The red shovel with the silver spade

scrapes a shallow trench, hard with drought.
I must dig deeper to keep away the strays.
I have wrapped her in a scrap of cloth,

slight goddess-named Phoebe who sounded
larger when she dove against the window
where I sat unconcerned, interred in thought

as one who sits alone & reads & drifts.
She was soft as a newborn's skin & warm
in my hands which petted her, glass-bright eyes

fixed like one who looks for stars in moonlight.
Was she a child or child's mother? A child,
I think, her lovely quiet chest dappled

below her throat like a stippled egg.
My grandmother wanted me a Phoebe,
a hand-me-down for someone

she must have loved or known.
But I ought to have been christened
the poet's young Margaret, heartsore,
this good grey Goldengrove buried, wept for.

Another Drought

After days & days of searing heat, Saturday arrives
blowsy, cool, & blue-eyed, almost springlike, a week
before the June solstice. How do the birds survive?
I consider the coyote who surprises us on the former

tram bed that runs behind the oaks near the road,
& the turkeys that roost in the neighborhood
& flap onto a gazebo roof, a couple of hens coaxing
a dozen fledges up & later down. Was the coyote near?

The forecasters say no rain for another week. We are bored
with all this sun & heat. Have you ever seen a crow pant?
It has a large beak & a pink tongue that quavers.
One day a storm blew through—five minutes

of moisture disappearing as it fell, reminding me
of our first summer here, & how I took the kids everywhere
to find moving air & cool water on sandy city beaches, or
up north to lakes with leeches & horseflies, & anywhere with air

conditioning because we only had fans, & at least once
to a movie after which I nearly cried because the suggestion
of a shower was evaporating on the hot pavement when we emerged
from the cool dark. That summer I didn't think of birds, coyotes,

or turkeys. I worried about acid rain, mercury in fish,
eggs with salmonella, & what food we could safely eat.

Meditation on Step Three

*~Made a decision to turn our will & our lives over
to the care of God as we understood God.*

At two sharp, the small, spotted tan & black service dog,
too small to be all shepherd, hurries the slight woman
holding its lead through the heavy glass push-and-it-will-open
door to the foyer of the central library, crowded with those
who have paused, & guides her past the next set
to the street. The animal slows when a balding man,
thin silver mane pulled into a long grey ponytail, matching
the faux fur collar on his coat, slowly approaches & touches
her arm. The dog's all business, no wagging or fawning
as the man walks ahead to a vehicle idling on the street.
When the van door slides open, the woman slips the lead,
& the business-like dog scrambles from curb to seat as
she feels for & opens the passenger door, settling herself.

Thrift

One day we were in a thrift store combing the racks
when Claire found a light pink & blue sack dress
with a sheer square panel sewn on the bodice, a posy
of tiny silk flowers tacked beneath. She ran her fingers
over the pane & on her face appeared what I only can describe
as a beatific smile forming at the corners of her mouth
as a faraway look came into her eyes.

It was like that just now when I looked closely
at the zinnias & Canadian goldenrod in the grey vase
centered in front of the dining window overlooking
the trees out back. No matter it's only a square of photo
on the computer desktop framed by a blue the color
of the sky. My eyes glazed as though it were the day
I gathered & arranged them on the glass-topped table.

There's a flower called thrift that grows on temperate
coasts around the world & on northern mountains
from Iceland to Siberia. It's near extinction in its colder habitat,
& fragile, but genetics has made it a household name, a plant
of many colors for rocky gardens, *Armeria maritima,* also known
as sea pink, lady's pin-cushion, sea thrift, cliff rose, sea gillyflower—
all cousins to the dainty flowers on Claire's beloved dress.

When I lived in Vermont, my friend Bridget & I would visit
the Salvation Army Thrift Store, the place her six-year-old daughter
called "The South of Asia," probably because of the war
in Vietnam, which hadn't yet ended. In a tabletop mound
of used clothing, I found a dark blue rayon dress with a colorful
flower print. The simple 50s dress looked beautiful when I
held it to the mirror & I was enchanted when I tried it on.

The Pencil
~A Brief History

A length of camel's hair, a small brush with a tail—
known as a little penis in the Medieval, it had a fine point
to make a fine line in a manuscript, a *pincel* to the French.

The *pincel* then became a seam of graphite,
& later still, was encased in wood, crude, but serviceable,
not unlike the modern pricey rainbow-colored kind

sheathed in a fat twig, a unique gift for someone
you hardly know or a person hard-to-buy-for.
Unwieldy, it will be set aside, forgotten.

Mine, six-sided, painted grey & orange,
has a vein of what used to be called lead,
& fits my hand the way I learned in school.

Cradled in the pocket between thumb & forefinger,
index pressing point to paper, it scrapes along
the page ciphering or lettering or drawing a vessel, say,

a ship carrying containers from overseas
that also carries pencils nestled in little boxes,
pencils & boxes made by children.

Erasure

~Vermont, Summer 2023

The end of summer & still it rains,
raining for months till streams have swollen.
Hillsides & bridges collapse, the water
flowing ever down, seeking its own desire.
On a rare day when blue sky & sun appear,
a monarch glues her pitch-black eggs,
small as poppy seeds, to the underseam
of a milkweed's stiff, sea green leaves.
Given a day or two, the edges are as jagged
as an elm's, eaten by half-a-dozen black & green
striped caterpillars that quickly swell in length
& breadth. A small one must have blown
onto the sidewalk from the fits & gusts
of last night's storm. If I could, I would return it
to its garden bed, but it has been crushed underfoot.
What remains is a dark smudge, any old thing.

Late Snow & the Birder Feeder

A fat junco flies in after
a night in the woods.
Large flakes eddy around him,
slide off as he flits away, coverts flashing.

He's the character actor, a portly comic
with spindly legs & delicate feet,
who moves with surprising agility.
A hawk, thinking himself the lead,

sweeps past, misses his cue & his meal.
He glowers on a limb offstage.
Two Sundays after Easter
there is no drama, no tragedy.

Sketches

~for Alveda & Valeria

I

When I first met them, they'd been friends
longer than I'd been alive, best friends since
childhood at the State Academy for the Deaf
in an era when children were parted from their families
for months at a time to learn a skill or trade,
like Val's husband Ray who became a printer,
& where they were taught not to use
their hands, only English & their voices.
It didn't work, the language part—most of the Deaf
I know write English unlike anything in a grammar book.

II

They counted among the "Strong Deaf"
at the church in Minneapolis where we took our family:
Minneapolis signed with a "D" for David,
a man who'd settled there early on. Deaf know
the city by a simple "D" repeated near the shoulder,
handed down like a priceless heirloom.

III

Alveda was a seamstress in a factory
for forty years & kept a Singer in an upstairs room
where she sewed clothes for her grandchildren
& matching outfits for my daughter & her dolls.
In her stiff & stifling living room she taught us Sign.

She must have feared her breath—always
a peppermint in her mouth. Before interpreters,
I played the part once when she saw her eye doctor.
At Christmas I took her shopping, but only at the organized
department store because her father had been a union man.
Her local son preferred Gold Toe socks. He wrote poetry.

IV

Sometimes we had lunch with the two widows
at the House of Wong on Sundays after church,
where they'd box a portion of their chop suey, & one
or the other might make the fifty-mile drive
with us to take Claire back to their old school
after a weekend home with her brother.

V

After Ray died, I drove Val to the cemetery to lay flowers
at his grave, reminding me of the Mason jar of zinnias
& volunteer snow-on-the-mountain left on my grandfather's.
She missed Ray. They'd had a happy marriage, whereas
Alveda dismissed her husband, who died
before I knew her, with a forceful, vocal *pah*.
Val's only child didn't sell the house
her mother was widowed in, nor live in it herself.
When I stop to visit Val's & Ray's plots, I see
Paulette has a stone next to theirs. I haven't touched
Alveda's though she's been dead fifteen years,
& I'm not sure where to find it.

VI

Toward the end, Val & I made a visit to the nursing home,
the only time, I think, I heard Alveda laugh, really laugh.
Both women's hands flew with the memory of being girls,
larking it up on their one big trip from Minnesota to San Francisco.
Dated ASL on arthritic fingers taxed my concentration,
& I forgot to ask how they got there, got back home.

As the Crow Flies

~for Ladybird, a Dog

Flakey, funny, insouciant, she tried to please,
        but never sat or stayed. Indignant, four-legged,
skittish shepherd mix, who didn't suffer her own kind,
        or any other creature, only the two-legged,
whom she loved unreservedly.

Claire signs your name each time we're together,
        adding the double-hand, half-dome word for grave,
& then the sign for collar, which we buried beneath the pines.
        I try to understand. Are her signs a litany
for loss & the blue sky where she plans to meet you?

You crashed the bed, peed the rug
        & couldn't walk or eat or hear the day we
took you in to see the vet, who saw my hesitation,
        felt free to offer that he'd brought his own old
dog back from strokes a dozen times.

Behind him & his needle, James shook his head, "No,"
        & scratched your ruff. I held your muzzle
in my lap, bidding you, Ladybird, our sweet Bird
        of the scarred nose & itchy rump—
god-speid.

Tankas & the Temperature

Yellow-rumped Warblers

Just when it seems they'll
never return, a dozen
butter-butts descend
en masse in search of inchworms
in Langton Lake's dying woods.

*Range is shrinking, as is
their ability to find insects
upon arrival from the tropics
after spring in the north is
well underway.*

Pileated Woodpecker

A jackhammer head
pounds at the frozen suet
nailed to the tree
at the bottom of the hill,
denting the cold slab.

*Habitat cleared for centuries.
Somehow, for now, they're
more common.*

Wood Duck

The flashy young male
huddled under the pine waits
for the big-eyed hen
to stroll from behind the trunk
in her herringbone coat.

*Too good-looking, tasty, habitat
shorn & with it, nesting holes, until
legal protection & nesting boxes
introduced. A warmer climate
threatenes additional stressors*

Cooper's Hawk

New chicks in last year's
rag-tag nest of small branches
with tree-bark lining.
How the parents have frightened
the songbirds into hiding!

*Despite DDT, etc., numbers hold
steady until the temperature rises.*

Cardinal

Did they harry it
to death? That strange-looking male
with the vulture's cap?
The one its rivals chased off
when its long-time mate decamped?

*Numbers stable in their range
east of the Rockies until pushed
further north from rising temps.*

Oriole

All eight, mostly young,
peck at the grape jelly spooned
from the Welch's jar.
Bright beauty first, then the old,
each brilliant eye gleaming black.

*By 2080, range will be as far north
as Alaska due to extreme heat.*

West Virginia: Pop Williams

~a pantoum

Too young to play ball in my grandmother's lot,
   I perched on Pop's knee for the after-supper games.
      He smelled the smell of a workingman's salt, & sweat
         damped his shirt with the tang of old cigarettes.

Those August evenings I sat content on his ample knee.
   He was squat & square, sparkplug-like, & kingly,
      his odor hovering in the rose humidity of the open field.
         My siblings' memories have fogged, no registry of him—

they had each other, but he was royalty to me.
   Sometimes he played horseshoes with the other men by the woods & river.
      What *do* the siblings remember if none of this?
         Did our grandfather play ringers with the men? They cannot say.

Like Pop, the other men were laborers who threw the relics
   of their farm days near the falling banks of the Monongahela river.
      My grandfather may have been another sort, tie tucked into his shirt.
         The games are clear, the men Pop played with indistinct.

That fertile field lies inert beneath lifeless asphalt: old horses, shoes, & all.
   The cries of bases stolen, ringers thrown, have died away.
      My mother would know about her father, but she is buried, too.
         All are gone, gone to where I cannot say–but flown.

Summer nights, shouting, laughter, timelessness
   when Pop Williams was alive & bumped me on his knee.
      No one else remembers what l can sense & see—
         twilight haze mixing dreamily with sweat & cigarettes.

Mirabile Dictu

Deep in a rotted hole in a chest-high
        post in a corner of the garden
lie six small speckled eggs as small
        as the end of my smallest finger,
so small & unexpected I can hardly breathe.
        After hoeing & planting, I dare
to look again. A chickadee huddles there,
        tail flanked against the post's rough wall,
& though her onyx eyes are open, she ignores me.
        I don't tell anyone what I've seen
& check the nest only now & then. I find
        a flat stone to shade part of
the opening from the sun. It's already
        a hot spring. One day I see her
dive in to brood the clutch. Days later,
        all the eggs have hatched. Naked
chicks with big beaks & bulging eyes lie
        haphazard—it looks like all six of them,
though it's hard to see. I'm as inconspicuous
        as a tall woman can be. Blind,
the young are covered in fine gray down.
        One open mouth, flanged
with white, cries for food. It hasn't rained
        in weeks. I spray the post,
hoping droplets will fall in. The babies
        grow feathers, begin to look
like chickadees. I worry how they'll
        fledge so deep a nest, but that's
a human thing. The next time I check,
        they're gone.

Spring Song

Yesterday morning's wind brought rain,
then storied clouds against a blue, blue sky,
clouds like castles that took my breath,
brighter clouds mushrooming, taking it again.

Afternoon, behind the budding trees, dark sky
glowered, washed with purple bruises
followed by a charging wind that clawed across the screen,
pelting lime-green grass with perlite hail.

Whipped clean, laundered, blued,
sent tripping eastward over the garages,
whistling that familiar of mid-western spring:
Whistling not, where are you going?
But *where?*

Where have you been?

III

Reservoir Woods in Low Light

It was the day of the St. Paul Christmas Count &
in the urban park between the reservoir & cemetery,
Juke called in a saw-whet from his phone,
& because the sky was overcast in the hour before dawn
I was able to make it out, a clump on a bare branch ten feet off.
I shone the light on it so both of us could see the little owl,
& held the beam a moment until Juke said, "Enough, we'll leave it alone now."
Then after breakfast returned to see what else there was to see.

Spring now in the same woods searching for warblers in the evening light,
but only redwings whistle in the bone-dry marsh,
its raffia-like reeds trampled flat by dogs & deer.
And in the middle of this one-time lake,
a stick & limb nest in the only tree, leaf-bare & dead for years,
holds four new eaglets, whose precious heads
bob & duck above the tilting mass, which next winter
will collapse under the heaviest snowfall on record.

Matrilineal

I

When I was born, someone I met just twice
made me a quilt by hand with nine white ducks

in squares on what is now, some seventy years later,
a faded green background. Each duck sits immobile

in one dimension & all, save one, sports an orange cap,
the color echoed in each splayed foot & broad bill.

I try to picture her, my grandmother, Sarah Ann, whose regard
is mostly hidden as she unfurls a bright green backing across

a wooden quilting frame. Rough batting, unrolled & smoothed,
& flecked with bits of cotton boll, concealed by the cloth of ducks—

all three layers stretched over a waist-high frame,
& joined with a fine stitch no bigger than a grain of rice.

Maybe she forgot the missing cap, but I find it improbable.
How could a seamstress as skilled as she forget a detail like that?

Did she run out of cloth, or did she believe only her creator could
make a perfect thing, like a feathery dreamcatcher, which I'm told

will harbor a single flaw? One Christmas she sent a lofty loaf
of white bread in a holiday box filled with what else I'll never know.

And once, she came to Buffalo when I was very young & sewed
a lipstick-plaid slipcover for the gray daybed tucked in my room.

II

Sarah Ann's mother, with whom I share a name & birthdate,
earned her passage as a cook on a transatlantic ship from Scotland.
The small mountain town where Sarah Ann was born in 1886 sounds
like the petaled *rhododendron,* but Rhodell, West Virginia, a mining town,

population 173 in 2010, was named for a coal man in 1910 when
the population in the valley was several hundred more. My mother
was likely pregnant when my parents eloped in '36, a source, I think,
of the chafing between my mother's mother & my father. The summer

after my sister was born, my parents spent a season with his family—
his drunken father, my father's younger siblings, & an outdoor privy—
all of which may further explain the distance, greater than miles, that
would come to separate the families, thanks, in part, to my mother's

city-woman sensibilities, if only collegiate Morgantown. Sarah Ann's
survival, my father's, too, depended on her independent wages,
& clarifies my father's duty in sending money home to her
after she was widowed. I would never get to know Sarah Ann,

nor the complexities of her life, a model of a kind, & was
on my own when she died in '73. And now, the ducks,
the perfect & imperfect, lie silent in the cedar chest in the living room,
& I haven't a notion who will want them when I die.

Rosemary

With curly jet-black hair, she was the prettiest girl in the fourth-grade,
& when she died before the holidays, my mother took me to the rite.
Ringlets framed her porcelain-white face, cheeks rouged pink,
& she lay quiet in the coffin in a Christmas-red dress with bright

smocking across the chest, her stockinged feet strapped
into black patent-leather Mary Janes. I couldn't see where
the tumor had been & don't recall other girls in the pews.
Rosemary hadn't been a friend; she'd missed too much school for that.

I didn't understand my mother's interest. I felt I was her excuse
or did she know some grief, her own, her brother's early death?
I never asked, just that the service wasn't in my family's church.
The way everyone doted on her form made me jealous

in childish way—I *was* a child! Afterward, I went to my room
& shut the door. I sat at the desk with the hidden bottom drawer
& wrote a rhyming poem about her parents, who'd been kind,
not blind to know she, whom death had claimed, was best.

Moving on from the Graveyard

Camouflaged & sinking, sea-dark stones—
Moss-topped, lichened, chiseled names obscured—
An invitation to envy the silent ones
Who have lain a century or more interred?
Overlooking a shadowy ravine,
Where daylight sieves leaf by veiny leaf—
The palmate maple, oak, mountain ash, & pine—
Sundry birds—fear, poverty, old grief—
Flit among the graves. Bottom heavy juncos,
Gray as tombs, & the ever-skittish jay,
Vivid wash of blue, pause wherever most
A headstone's handy, piloting the way.
        One thinks to follow them—but have a care—
        The docent gardener may stop, then stare.

Legacy

They call them skins, the disemboweled bodies of birds stored
in the flat drawers of natural history museums around the world.

When white settlers headed west, there were so many red-headed
woodpeckers from Maine to Minnesota that no one bothered

to count or study them. Ornithologist & artist John James Audubon
had the habit of killing the birds he drew, then gutting & stuffing them

for his life studies—so many birds everywhere in America, it hardly
mattered in the early 1800s. He probably furnished many European

museums, including pelts of New World mammals like the swift fox,
otter, badger to European collectors to raise money to feed his often

poverty-stricken family. He likely invented the "Bird of Washington"
to increase sales of *The Birds of America*, his magnum opus, which cost

around $2,000,000 to print in today's currency. From the late nineteenth
century into the early twentieth, many decried the killing of birds

for sport, as the demise of the once-ubiquitous passenger pigeon
made clear; in 1950's Florida, my husband may have shot ivorybills,

now thought extinct, with a BB gun in the swampy woods around
his boyhood home, the Strawberry Capital of the World.

Harry Runner & the Horse

The Greek *metaphorein*, to carry, transcends to metaphor,
& in nineteenth century novels led to the sturdy horse,
a natural carrier of meaning when it leapt a fence
or thudded down in the middle of a love affair
or at the beginning of the end of one,
just as a horse may have carried my grandfather, Harry,
on the family farm by the Monongahela river,
where my mother was born & grew up,
& where Harry lived until the middle of the last century,
just after the second war, & where he died,
on the same parcel, in the same place,
& where by then there were no horses,
just a falling-down barn & two fields on either side
of an ancient house whose yellow paint was flaking.

In the bowed-glass secretary on the second floor,
an 1877 copy of *Ray's New Practical Arithmetic*
survived Harry, who doodled in the margins
& called William Jennings Bryan a hobo.
The manual's sepia pages abound in not so simple math
featuring horses & other agrarian equations,
as well as an adage Harry penciled about "loving many,
trusting few," & "always paddling your own cano [*sic*]."
One problem begins, "A farmer sends
to a dealer 20 horses and 15 mules to be sold."
Another figures both a horse & a carriage,
& I suppose Harry traveled that way, though his father,
Lewis Moore, who left before Harry could remember,
probably rode off on a train north to Erie.

Harry, or Poppy, whom I was too young to know,
but long to have, a gentle man by all accounts,
came from a line of German Läufers, whose name
meant to run, *better to run than to loaf,*
& those first people changed it to Runner
so long ago my second oldest sister can't tease
the records further, nor can she trace Harry's blood
in the family tree, & that is a mystery she won't
explore, or maybe can't unless she has Harry dug up
& tested, & Lewis Moore, too, because he eventually
came home, & even though I think my sister dearly
believes that blood is thicker than water, I'm on
the fence because of my love of both water & of
thoroughfares, & she, in want of clarity, fears he won't be ours.

West Virginia: Song

How I loved the mountains of my childhood,
mountains that rose along the lazy Monongahela,
mountains that sweltered in summer
& were barren in the faint snow of winter.

How I loved the long gray porch where I
read on a worn green swing, alone because
I was youngest & forgotten that way. And
the railroad tracks & the trains, brimming

coal from mines somewhere not too far,
engines with smokestacks fuming like grim-faced
men in black hats that roared as they passed,
toothy-grinned, black grills protruding.

And the barges on the river carting more coal,
& the tugboats that cajoled them along until
they reached the locks & dam. How could I
not love it all, being so smitten? But mostly,

I loved the house with its high ceilings, glass
transoms, worn rugs, tables, china, untuned piano,
& knotted floorboards on the second story,
where I was put to bed early in a hot

& breathless room, unable to sleep because
of the heat & wanting to be with my mother,
grandmother, & the great aunts whose
unhurried gossip rose from the porch below.

Claire: Mother's Day

The ninth of May, just days into spring, & there they were
arguing with her on the top floor of the hospital overlooking
the freeway in a room filled with heavy furniture.
For the matter of logic: The ward was double-locked.
Her room was standard, single metal bed bolted to the floor,
bathroom, no colors, tile floor. She'd met us at the door
without niceties— *i want to go home! i don't like it here!*
i want to go home! take me home now!!! in vehement ASL.
The psychiatric resident doctor appeared, his weekend shift
about over, & a pharmacist, too, both nice looking guys,
but neither could sign, complicating things.
They'd changed her drugs, told us the names, effects.
What about the old ones? *These are better,* they said.
You can tell over three days? *She has to go back to her*
group home tomorrow. We can't keep her any longer, they said.
When she understood she couldn't leave with us, she threw
the boxy TTY for making phone calls against the fixed table.
Silent attendants hurried us to the door with unsettling speed.

My Mother's Hands

My mother's hands,
folded on her chest
as she rests, supine,
listening to her books

for the blind.
My own hands, folded
when I lie down to sleep:
now veined, skin thinned

like hers, the palmate
bones showing through.
Hers, in her last days
on the respirator,

folded the same, &
in the box at church,
her last home.
She, my first

home, where
folded inside
her belly,
I began.

Man with a Hatchet
~Liliana Porter

Porter has said her installation in a third-floor gallery in Buenos Aires,
her homeland's capital, is about destruction & regeneration.
Said destruction begins on a nearly room-sized, tiered white box

with a miniature man holding a hatchet frozen above his head
at the source of a long, ever-widening river of broken cups, plates,
dollhouse chairs, detritus of the twentieth century that spill across

the flat white surface. Carmine sand floods another area where a miniature
woman in a green skirt grooms the sand with a wide-toothed rake, like
Sisyphus with his boulder, each day a forever, or a blunt reminder of a female's

post-menarcheal life. Between & around these streams lie dolls' heads,
jumbled toys, the Kennedy limousine just before, then Jackie climbing wildly,
blindly, a group of snipers, tin soldiers, a deconstructed harmonium,

springs sprung, black keys worn, white keys discolored, & Che Guevara
pictured on a smashed commemorative plate beside a heap of golden BBs.
Does La Liliana believe a small ceramic speckled fawn nestled by the harmonium,

some pretty flowered plates, though broken, & a sea of blue net knit by
another tiny woman precariously seated on the edge of one tier are
emblematic of hope, the way the eruption of Mt. St. Helens gave way to

bountiful growth? Left to ponder what the small woman trudging across
the white surface is carrying in her shiny brown suitcase, I decide
it holds a map, a compass, a gas mask, & packets of seeds to plant
whenever she arrives—wherever she may be heading.

Counting Horses

First there were two, then over the years, four.
Now, eight ham-hooved, colossal yellow horses
close by the county road to the School for the Deaf.
Shoulder to shoulder, they stand in placid pairs,
stolid Belgians, even the young massive,

though in miniature, & not for long.
I count them when I drive the back road,
counting them the way sixty years ago we counted
roadside cows & horses to pass the time.
Sometimes at the fair, I've seen these blinkered,

pulling hay, or at a parade, clumping,
hauling a field or fire wagon full of country girls.
Today they breathe in gusts & swells.
They are beautiful in their muddy paddock,
all eight in two's, standing sleeping, in snow

or rain, & when the orchard's all pink petals,
then apple cider, pumpkins, scarecrows.
Seasons long the horses stand. My girl is grown.
The Deaf School done these many years.

The Opera Rocks

So called because they resemble nothing so much as three sails inflated by a tailwind like the vaulted & vaunted opera house in Sydney Harbour, the Opera Rocks on Islay are metamorphic brown-black, upturned, & covered by emerald grass in places, known as Smaull in an earlier age, the highest of which goes by Dun Bheolain, *Bheolain* supposedly the name of a prehistoric chieftain, & *dun*: "a stone-built fortified settlement in Scotland or Ireland, of a kind built from the late Iron to the early Middle Ages," where such fortifications endured years of Viking raids & internecine warfare. And, indeed, there is evidence of a prehistoric fort on one rock, protected by steep cliffs on three sides & once upon a time by a wall of stone & turf on the southeastern face, now become but green depressions that look like places the bodies of men could crouch in & use not stone or bronze weapons to defend their families & sheep, but heavy swords of the latest iron or steel, sturdier, & presumably more dangerous in a time before black powder, & ages before guns, rifles, & other deadly weapons. Because I am woman I try to imagine a woman's life in what was surely a damp & squalid place, where what warmth she found arose from turf flame & the filthy fleece of wild sheep whose coarse wool she spun & wove to wrap herself & infants in, where early death from pregnancy & raw subsistence were constant in attendance, a rugged place a woman might not survive or flee, charmingly tagged today for an opera house half-a-world away.

Robin's Egg Blue

It's a luxury to write
about a bird, any bird, when
the world is full of anguish,
especially this bird, so fearless
or feckless that it will build a nest
anywhere, even in plain sight,
such as in the cleft of an unleafed
tree outside a friend's window,
where after four days, four eggs
are laid, one each day, the color
its own particular shade of blue.
The female sat on them throughout
a late spring snow until the hatchlings
pecked their way to light in the cup
of twigs cemented with mud from
a cloud of dirt dust & puddle water.
They have flown by now, or should have,
& the parents, unable not to trust the future,
will use their one-time home to brood
more eggs, & further sets of wings, no matter.

In Holland

~for my husband

Years & we couldn't speak,
yet here where words are foreign,
I listen as though an ocean has cleansed us.
We walk in fine damp air
awed by the newness of old things—
buildings, a bricked path, or a
common pasture on the way to town
where five cows, milk bags slapping,
chase in perfect disorder their five spotted calves,
all leaping as though over the fabled moon.
Later among canals & farms
we hold hands, watch nesting godwits
whose flight from Africa brings them here
where they make their homes among
grazing herds, friends.

West Virginia: Landscape

My father liked to find a country road, drive
to its end, then head back home, like a bird
sensing a magnetic field, or a honeybee its hive.
What was it that he sought? To see the seams
of shiny coal, the varied trees he taught me to name,
the fireflies coming down the mountainsides in drifts
of light? Or was it the flame-red cardinals he said had lost
their luster since he was young, or as he claimed, to hear
again the Elizabethan cadences in an isolated holler?
After my mother died, I visited his stony silence
three or four times a year. Once, he had me drive
into the Virginia countryside to find a man
he remembered sold good tomatoes.
Somehow we found the place, a nearby town
far behind us, down a winding road. Then he led
the two of us back home, where my mother
wasn't there to cook up the soup we loved.

On the Occasion of Your Birthday
~for Elizabeth at Ninety-Five

The day began
damp & cool, overcast,

blue-patched—Dutchman's britches
in the old almanac—

but soon was limpid, all sun & wind,
warm & cloudless.

Out-of-doors this evening,
we watched dark clouds roll in,

then grow roseate,
auspicious before embarking—

a prophecy for you, dear friend,
& us, as well.

Swans at Lake Johanna

Those white flags flashing on the lake
aren't flags at all, but long-necked swans
gleaming in the tannin-dark shallows,
their garbled gabbling nothing like trumpets
for which a birder says they're named,
who also says a warm long fall
has sustained the weeds they tear at
when they sink their heads & slender necks
beneath the marbled water
so beautifully,
oblivious that their twenty are a wonder
on a November afternoon short of light.

NOTES

"Handbook on Grief" takes its title from *The Grief Handbook: A guide through the worst days of your life* by Bridget McNulty, Watkins Publishing 2021.

"For Stan" is for Stanley Plumly, who died of multiple myeloma in 2019, & who was the Maryland Poet Laureate & Distinguished University Professor at the University of Maryland.

Several lines from Hayden Carruth's poem, "Essay," are echoed in the poem, "Urban Pond."

"Phoenixbirds" is based on a letter Ken Kesey wrote to friends following the tragic death of his son & can be found in the book *Letters of Note: Grief* by Shaun Usher, published by Penguin Books, an imprint of Penguin Publishing Group, a division of Penguin Random House, LLC. Copyright © 2022 by Shaun Usher.

"The Phoebe" recalls the poem "Spring and Fall: to a young child" by Gerard Manley Hopkins. https://www.poetryfoundation.org/poems/44400/spring-and-fall.

"Erasure" was conceived during the rains & flooding in Ripton, Vermont, August 2023.

Climate predictions in "Tankas & the Temperature" are sourced from Audubon.org, ClimateAdaptationExplorer.org, & DataBasin.org.

Many of the facts about J. James Audubon in "Legacy" are from the Audubon Society of America, JohnJames.Audbon.org, & Wikipedia.

"Harry Runner & the Horse" is informed by the article "The Horse: Beloved Metaphor of Your Favorite 19th-Century Novelists" by Ulrich Raulff, *LitHub*, February 12, 2018. Ray's *New Practical Arithmetic* was published in 1877 by the American Book Company.

In "Claire: Mother's Day," TTY is an acronym for TeleTYpe, consisting of a keyboard & a place to attach a telephone receiver. They are not in common use today.

"Man with a Hatchet" is based on an installation by artist Liliana Porter in Buenos Aires in 2014 at *Malba Exposiciones*.

"The Opera Rocks" was inspired by the blogger Fhithich, Scots for raven. Quoted definition is from the Oxford Online Dictionary. To see a photo of the rocks, go to: http://www.fhithich.uk/?p=28100.

ACKNOWLEDGEMENTS

Gyroscope: "Phoenixbirds"; *Nimrod International Journal*: "Cloud," "Inheritance," "Reverie at the other Como"; *SALT*: "Paper-Whites"; *SIEVA*: "The Phoebe."

Special Thanks to:

Gretchen Marquette, beloved mentor & author of *May Day* (Gray Wolf Press, 2015).

The Bread Loaf Writers Conference.

The Loft Literary Center.

Kiki Theodoropolous, who said I hadn't lost my touch.

The many friends, family, & fellow writers who listened to or read these poems over many years.

My children, James & Claire.

And, especially my husband Dick Levins, the best.

About the Author

Jane Dickerson's previous collection, *The Orange Tree: Early Poems (2015),* was a finalist for the Midwest Independent Publishing Association Award. She earned an MFA from the University of Maryland, where she won The Academy of American Poets Prize. She has contributed twice at the Bread Loaf Writers' Conference in Vermont. She is also a mentor for the Minnesota Prison Writers Workshop and works as a freelance editor in St. Paul, Minnesota.

www.ingramcontent.com/pod-product-compliance
Lightning Source LLC
Chambersburg PA
CBHW020332090426
42735CB00009B/1511